M&A in Pharma: A Growing Trend

October 2019

EUREKA! Consulting Solutions Limited
Registered Address:
7 Bell Yard,
WC2A 2JR London
United Kingdom
www.eureka.consulting
info@eureka.consulting

Table of Contents

Executive Summary 3
Introduction 5
1. **Conceptual Framework** 7
   1.1   Types of Mergers & Acquisitions 7
   1.2   The Empirical Results 8
   1.3   Six Archetypes for Value-Creation 10
   1.4   Common reasons why M&A's fail 11
2. **M&A in the Pharmaceutical Industry** 13
   2.1   Pharmaceutical Industry overview 13
   2.2   The Drivers behind the Moves 16
   2.3   Acquisition Premia in Pharma 18
   2.4   Six Factors that contribute to Success in Pharma 19
   2.5   Key Trends and Challenges ahead 20
3. **Case Analysis: GSK Consumer Healthcare** 22
   3.1   History of the Alliance 23
   3.2   The Partner Companies 24
   3.3   The Basis of the Strategic Alliance 27
   3.4   Financial Considerations 28
   3.5   Main Benefits and Synergies 32
   3.6   Principal Risks and Uncertainties 34
Conclusions 36
Bibliography 38
Appendices 42

Executive Summary

Until the end of the last century, organisations had been looking for ways to increase their profitability or obtain competitive advantage by benefiting from market failure or implementing economy of scale strategies. Nowadays, with the advent of globalization, this practice has changed and companies have started looking at acquiring other firms or merge with them in order to ensure **business sustainability** and **continuous growth**.

Today, Mergers and Acquisitions (**M&A**) are often considered the most efficient and rapid way for organisations to transform their business and keep up with a constantly changing environment. And, because of the pressure from globalisation, companies will continue to pursue these opportunities in order to remain fruitful and innovative regardless of market fluctuations and economic variations.

In this regard, the pharmaceutical industry is probably one of the first that comes to mind. Over the past twenty years or so, the concept of scale economy along with the need of continuously pursuing technological innovation have become more and more prominent in the Pharma world. A **growing trend** has been observed in this industry in the recent years, with an increasing number of mergers and acquisitions taking place across all geographies and therapeutic areas, thanks to a particularly favourable Regulatory environment, convenient interest rates and important tax reforms. Among the key drivers also the need to reduce the high costs of research and development, the desire to enter new markets and to fight competition.

The case of the new **GSK Consumer Healthcare** organisation, from the merger of the two Consumer Healthcare divisions from the British firm GlaxoSmithKline and the American Pfizer, is further analysed in this document to summarise the events leading to the creation of a new global pharmaceutical giant, while inviting the reader to consider the process of growth through M&A and driving their attention towards some of the critical aspects to consider during the evaluation of a deal.

For decades academics and other researchers have studied the question of whether acquisitions do create value. The empirical evidence presented in this paper is important because it helps the reader understand that there is no mathematical formula that can help predict if a deal will be successful in the end. Each M&A opportunity must have its own **strategic rational** and the organisations involved in the process must ensure they have the necessary skills to translate strategy into action.

The benefits of such transactions are many, but so are the challenges they bring to organisations. Buyers today are concerned with the level of prior due diligence to be performed, the extent of risk of compliance or reputation, costs of integration, timetable and so on. Sellers face similar challenges that equally require close attention.

Despite the hurdles, companies particularly in the pharmaceutical industry cannot ignore M&A strategies as a mean to growth. The '**right deal**' can help offset the challenges companies face as the result of the increase in regulatory complexity, the rise of competition, price pressures or lack of innovation. If the acquisition is aligned with the broader strategy of the business and appropriate measures are taken before and after the transaction, a company can go hunting for targets with confidence. Deals hit the mark when they enable value creation not only for the shareholders but also for all stakeholders involved in the end-to-end process, including investors, employees, physicians, distributors and patients among others.

Ultimately, the objective of this book is not to draw conclusions on what is or is not a good deal, but to give the reader a comprehensive picture of the several strategic reasonings behind mergers and acquisitions and the most critical aspects to consider during a deal evaluation.

The overall landscape for the years ahead gives a very complex picture, however we can confidently believe that those who will have the ability to read through this complexity and execute sound M&A strategies in a structured and pragmatic manner as a result, will have greater chances to become sustainable and continue to grow in future.

I hope you find this document a useful and enjoyable read.

Valeria Graffeo, MPHARM MBA
Founder, Managing Director and Principal Consultant
EUREKA! Consulting Solutions Limited

Introduction

Mergers and **acquisitions** are often seen by enterprises as an opportunity to overcome some of the challenges that business operations bring, may that be technological development, financial constraints or commercial supremacy over competition (*Mittra, 2007*). Through well-planned strategic moves, companies may have the ability to obtain significant benefits, such as mitigation of business risks or the increase of profits or market share, hence why such tools have nowadays become of greater importance in the business practice.

The pharmaceutical industry is probably one of the first that comes to mind when we think about M&A, for various reasons. Over the past twenty years or so, the concept of scale economy along with the need of continuously pursuing technological innovation have become more and more prominent in the world of pharmaceuticals (*Lodorfos and Boateng, 2006*). In this context, the possibility of merging or acquiring a company have become a key aspect to consider in order to ensure **business sustainability** and **growth** over time (*Demirbag et al., 2007*).

A number of **large deals** can be found in support to this theory by looking only a few years back. For example, in 2015 AbbVie, a leading global biopharmaceutical company, acquired Pharmacyclics, a cancer and immune-disease focused enterprise, for US$ 21 billion[1]; in 2016 Shire, a leading biotech company focussed on rare diseases, acquired Baxalta, a biopharmaceutical company specialising in bleeding disorders, for US$ 32 billion[2] and in 2017 Johnson & Johnson completed the acquisition of the Swiss biotech Actelion, a global biopharmaceutical company focussed on innovative drugs for high unmet medical needs, for US$ 30 billion[3]. And this trend does not seem to be slowing down: according to the law firm Baker McKenzie, M&A in the Pharmaceutical sector increased by 50% in 2018, with North America accounting for more than half of the transactions, reaching a 18-year record of US$ 3.2 trillion. This happened after a year (2017) where drug approvals from Food And Drug Administration (FDA) Agency, the competent authority responsible in the United States, hit a 21-year record with 46 new chemical entities receiving the green light for commercialisation and an increasing number of new products developed from young biotech companies was recorded. Another important factor that highly influenced this growing trend in 2018 was the the 'Tax Cuts and Jobs Act' in the United States, a major revamp of fiscal rules which influenced dealmakers' strategies towards expansion, signed in December 2017.

A **Regulatory environment** open to welcoming technological innovation, along with convenient **interest rates** and **tax reforms** that encourage entrepreneurship, create the right context for mergers and acquisitions and help shape how enterprises plan and fund their acquisitions. "Companies with money overseas can now reach out to global capital and acquire more easily" said the investment fund Case Equity Partners, although American bankers claim that the recent tax reform in the US would have had only a limited impact on the negotiations.

With the considerably **high costs of research and development** in Pharmaceuticals as well as the **expiry of patents** on blockbuster products, mergers and acquisitions may sometimes represent the best if not 'the only option' to bring in additional revenue. Furthermore, the pressure on prices in areas such as diabetes and respiratory diseases, are pushing companies to look at **niche areas** of disease, where biotechnology does excel. Thus, for large pharmaceutical companies as well as those with a strong biotech vocation, small and innovative startups became a vital source of experimental drugs with which to integrate internal pipelines.

---

[1] Sourced from "The biggest pharmaceutical company takeovers in 2015", pharmaceutical-technology.com

[2] Sourced from "12 biggest mergers and acquisitions of 2016", fortune.com

[3] Sourced from "Pharmaceutical M&A deals in 2017", thepharmaletter.com

However, what sometimes gets lost in the process are two of the most critical activities which must be conducted prior to beginning the M&A process, **strategic research** and **due diligence**. As described by Bain & Company in one of their case analysis ("*Six ways to make healthcare deals work", 2010*), for a successful acquisition it is essential that clear guidelines are set at the very early stages of the process. Furthermore, there seems to be common practices such as valuing both internal and external sources of innovation or maintaining a regular pace of M&A activity to mention a couple, that if followed by the acquiring companies are luckily to increase the chances of success in a deal. Furthermore, a Survey conducted by PwC in 2018 with 600 senior corporate executives shows that, contrarily to what initially supposed, many acquisitions and divestments 'do not maximize value'. This is because some aspects which significantly undermine the value created, for example failing to plan for cultural change or develop a knowledge retention and risk mitigation plan, are often under-estimated by companies during the integration process. Instead, companies that genuinely prioritise value creation over pure financials and avoid to fall into the false assumption that integration will occur as a natural consequence of the M&A process itself, have a considerably higher chances to **maximise value** in a deal ("*Value creation deals", PwC*).

The objective of this paper is to analyse the different aspects that characterise mergers and acquisitions in order to help the reader build a broader perspective of the subject and form their own opinion around what critical questions to ask when evaluating a deal.

1. Conceptual Framework

Mergers and acquisitions (M&A) nowadays can be considered a critical component of a vigorous economy. At various stages of the life span of a company, some business decisions that had strategic sense once, may no longer do at another point. For example, a company that patented a ground breaking innovation at some stage may not be able to exploit it without making though decisions that change the course of things. In these circumstances, mergers and acquisitions may often be the best way to reallocate resources rapidly and wisely.

In general terms, acquisitions that reduce inefficiencies or put organisations under better managers or owners are typically those that create the most considerable value for the company as well as for its investors, or at least this is what combined cash flows show for most of the companies involved in this type of transactions as T. Killer, M. Goedhart and D. Wessels point out in their number 1 best-selling guide to corporate valuation ("*Valuation – Measuring and Managing the Value of Companies*", 2015) from which the theory presented in this section is mainly taken.

In financial terms, we can say that an acquisition has created value for companies when the 'cash flows' of the merged entities are higher than what they would have if the transaction did not take place. This value can be estimated as follows:

Value Created for the Acquirer = Value Received - Price Paid

For clarity, the 'value received' by the acquiring company in this formula is equal to the 'intrinsic value' of the company being acquired as if it was a separate entity, plus the 'present value' of what can be reached post-acquisition through the implementation of **performance improvements** and **other synergies**; the 'price paid' is the 'market value' of the company being acquired increased by a 'premium' which may be necessary in order to influence the shareholders of the acquired company towards selling their shares.

With this in mind, we can come to the conclusion that, if the cost of such improvements necessary to increase the operating performance of the company are greater than the premium paid to convince the shareholders of the target company, the deal is not creating value.

Due to the number of variables that contribute to the final output, including but not limited to the cultural differences between the merging companies which may affect the speed and quality of the integration process for instance as discussed later on in this paper, the ability to **quantify the synergies** in order to determine the appropriate value attributable to the improved operating performance following M&A's remains one of the most challenging aspect to gauge. At the same time, it is among the most influential to be taken into account, therefore it cannot be neglected.

1.1 Types of Mergers & Acquisitions

In business, the terms mergers and acquisitions are often used interchangeably and at times in an incorrect way also. This is because there are some differences between the two terms which indicate two different types of transactions: in very simple terms, while **merger** means 'to combine', **acquisition** means to 'acquire'; therefore mergers refer to the combination of 2 or more businesses who join their forces to form a brand new entity, acquisitions instead occur when a company takes control of another.

Both mergers and acquisitions are primarily classified in horizontal, vertical and mixed. The difference among the three lies primarily on the scope or ultimate objective which the combining firms intend to achieve through the transaction:

- **Horizontal** mergers and acquisitions are those where the primary objective is either to gain 'market share or price by reducing the number of competitors that manufacture or sell the same product(s) in the market and/or to increase their scale economies (*Clougherty and Duso, 2009: 1368; Pilsbury and Meaney, 2009*).

- **Vertical** mergers and acquisitions are those in which companies that operate in the same industry but at different stages of the process, for example a manufacturer and a supplier. The intent behind this class of mergers is mainly to reduce the costs of production and also increase profits by improving internal efficiencies, thus to obtain cost advantages, improve adaptability to changes in the market, become stronger in a competitive environment, benefit from the effect of synergy or else access the raw materials in a timely manner and under more convenient conditions (*Harrigan, 2003*).

- Lastly, in **mixed** mergers and acquisitions (also known as conglomerate) the companies merging are not competitors in the same market, nor the output of either of the companies involved in the transaction is used in the production process of the other as an input (*Church, 2008*). As the result of this, the challenges experienced in horizontal and vertical mergers are not observed because there is no relation in production or competition between the merging companies (*Wang & Chiu, 2013*). In general, mixed mergers are used by the acquiring company to enter new markets or geographies as well as a way to diversify and mitigate risks or to maximise the financial capacity (*Morresi & Pezzi, 2014*).

The most common M&A's seen in the pharmaceutical industry are the horizontal mergers as opposed to vertical mergers which are the less frequently occurring type of merger in this industry (*Katsanis, 2015*). As thoroughly analysed and discussed in the upcoming chapters of this paper, providing capital for other R&D activities, achieving scale economies and increasing commercial opportunities, along with the need to fight the high competition which exists in this industry (*Dermibag et al., 2007*) are among the key factors to drive companies towards M&A's in this sector, as further explained in the next chapter.

1.2 The Empirical Results

Historical data related to M&A Activities taking place from 1968 to 2013 in U.S. and Europe shows a sensible increase in number and value of transactions over the past 50 years. This phenomenon has reached a peak of approximately US$ 4,500 billion inflation-adjusted value in 2007 prior to a slight decrease due to the economic downturn experienced in the global economy in the subsequent years (*Dealogic Database, 2013*). And today, this trend does not seem to be slowing down.

The literature around the topic of M&A is vast and the business cases studied in the attempt to identify common patterns among deals are plenty. For decades academics and other researchers have studied the question of whether acquisitions create value. To date, most of research provides evidence that acquisitions do '**create value**' for the collective shareholders (that is the acquiring company as well as the acquired one combined) and the broader economy, as shown for example by a research performed by McKinsey on 1,770 acquisitions taking place between 1999 to 2013 ("*Global M&A : Fewer Deals, Better Quality*", D. Cognman, 2014) whereby the combined value

of the acquirer and target company was estimated on average to have raised by 5.8% through some combination of cost and revenue synergies.

However, the information coming from certain sources may sometimes appear to be in conflict with the conclusion that the most of M&A activities may bring more value to the economy of a company. For instance, a study carried out by McKinsey in 2010 showed that only 1/3 of transactions in scope of the research exercise created value for the company, 1/3 did not and for the other 1/3 the results were inconclusive and therefore could not be accounted ("*A Strong foundation for M&A in 2010*", W. Rehm and C. Siversten).

Furthermore, some empirical studies focussing on the effect of M&A announcements on capital markets demonstrate that the average large deals (weighted by value) lower the acquire's stock price between 1 and 3% and same do stock returns following the acquisition ("*Do Shareholders of acquiring firms gain from acquisitions?*", S.B. Moeller, F.P. Schlingemann, R.M. Stultz, 2003). In their article, Mitchel and Stafford have observed that acquirers underperform their peers on shareholders returns by 5% over the 3 years after the acquisition ("*Managerial decisions and long-term stock price performance*", M.L. Mitchel and E. Stafford, Journal of Business, 2000).

Other results coming from empirical research demonstrate that 1/3 of the acquiring companies do not create value for their shareholders since the advantages of the acquisition are predominantly transferred to the shareholders of the selling companies. The challenge managers face when involved in these type of transactions is therefore to make sure they fall among those acquisitions that indeed 'create value' for their own shareholders. Based on the observations from these studies, it becomes obvious to conclude that the distribution of the value created appears to be sometimes unbalanced. As a matter of fact, the majority of the 'value created' by large transactions is distributed to the shareholders of the selling company, since on average they are receiving high premiums (usually around 30%) compared to the market price of their stocks prior to the announcement ("*Valuation – Measuring and Managing the Value of Companies*", T. Killer, M. Goedhart, D. Wessels 2015).

As pointed out by as T. Killer, M. Goedhart and D. Wessels most studies focus on the 'stock-price reaction' to acquisition announcements, however one consequence of this approach to be aware of is that large acquisitions tend to dominate the results thus causing a slight distortion of the outcome.

To overcome the bias of large acquisitions of the studies described above, researchers have looked at acquisitions programs run by certain companies rather than single acquisitions. In the study run by W. Rehm, R. Uhlaner and A. West ("*Taking a longer-term look at M&A value creation*", 2012), 639 'non-banking' companies from 1999 and 2010 were examined and grouped into 5 categories as follows:

- 'Programmatic', in other words acquirers who completed many acquisitions which amounted to a large percentage of their market capitalisation
- 'Tactical', i.e. those acquirers who also completed many deals, with a small percentage of their market capitalisation
- 'Large-deal', which are companies that completed at least one deal that was larger than 30% of the acquiring company's value
- 'Organic', i.e. companies who conducted almost no M&A activity, and
- 'Selective', representing those acquirers not falling into any of the categories above.

The result of this research showed that the programmatic, tactical and organic companies all exceeded their peers in terms of total returns to shareholders. The large-deal companies underperformed, in line with the expectation from the announcement-effect studies. Therefore, it was concluded that M&A's if executed correctly tend to be associated with **outperformance**.

If we bring our attention to the Pharmaceutical Industry, studies carried out on companies who have participated in M&A activities in this sector demonstrate that such types of transactions are mainly driven by the benefits of **scale economy**, the **increase of total turnover** and the **decrease of total R&D expenses** as

9

compared to the total figures that both enterprises made on their own prior to the transaction (*Haberberg and Rieple, 2008; Anderson et al., 2013; Depamphilis, 2012*).

For example, in 2006 Cilhoroz et al. performed an assessment of the the effect of revenues generated as the result of M&A activity in some large pharmaceutical companies over R&D expenses, by comparing 'pre- and after-deal' revenues and R&D costs of those organisations in scope of the study. This includes companies such as Roche & Genentech, Sanofi & Aventis, Merck&Co and Schering Plough who had incurred in some M&A activity over the ten year period between 1998 and 2014. The impact of these activities on the performance of the companies was analyzed by reviewing changes of certain parameters (that is sale revenues, profitability, etc.) before and after the merger had taken place. According to the results of this study, the M&A activity had created value for the enterprises in scope through the generation of funds that could be used to support their expensive R&D activities (*Cilhoroz et al., 2006*), a very important aspect close to the heart of any acquirers in this industry.

1.3 Six Archetypes for Value-Creation

Despite the number of studies performed in this area, the empirical research to date remains unable to identify specific M&A strategies that support the creation of value for the companies involved. This is mainly because acquisitions come in a wide variety of shapes and sizes and also because there is no objective way to classify acquisitions by strategy. However, in absence of empirical research, we can rely on the information produced by the experts in M&A strategies who have assisted companies from different industries going through this process to explore the primary circumstances that enable the creation of a favourable environment for deals to succeed and whether there are any patterns to success which can be observed from experience.

In their book "Valuation – Measuring and Managing the Value of Companies", T. Killer, M. Goedhart and D. Wessels from which the theory presented in this section is mainly taken, have suggested that the strategic rational for an acquisition that creates value typically fits in 1 of the 6 archetypes that follow:

- Improving the performance of the acquired organisation
- Consolidating in order to remove 'excess capacity' from their sector
- Creating 'market access' for the products of the acquired company
- Acquiring technologies, competences or skills more rapidly or at lower cost than they would if those were built 'in-house'
- Exploiting the scalability of a business
- Identifying potential innovators early and help them expand their businesses.

Experience suggests that if an acquisition does not fall at least in one of the above listed archetypes, it is not very likely it will create value in the end. The strategic rationale behind an acquisition should be articulated around one or more of these archetypes and be translated into something **sound and tangible** for the businesses involved.

The valuation process of a M&A deal indeed brings challenges and complexity. Besides the financial considerations which must be made upfront, there is a lot of non-financial aspects that are important when looking at a M&A deal. As anticipated in the first section, quantifying the synergies that a merger brings to the parent companies is key in order to determine the likelihood of success in creating value for the shareholders and the business as a whole. However, since variables are many, the challenges that this exercise bring are augmented. Hence, it may be useful to learn also about the most common pitfalls where others have fallen into in the past and how to avoid the most frequent common reasons why M&A fail.

1.4   Common reasons why M&A's fail

According to the "Financial Times Press" book, many research studies performed over the past few decades show that only half of the mergers are successful in the end and the overall rate of failure sits approximately around 50%.

Failure to produce and execute a comprehensive integration plan, lack of establishing appropriate level of controls, losing focus are only a few of the reasons which can lead to failure. Investopedia, where the information below is mainly taken from, has put together a list of the most common reasons for failure identified in M&A transactions along with some potential solutions to overcome these issues ("*Top reasons why M&A deals fail*", S. Seth, 2019):

- 'Little or no owners' involvement': Particularly in mid to large-size deals, it is often common practice among companies to engage M&A Advisory firms or large consulting businesses with specific skills and competences when dealing with this level of complexity. However, leaving the entire process in the hands of a third party seems to be one of the most common reasons for failures. This may be justified by the fact that the consulting firm may not have full insight into the business processes or the culture of an organisations to deeply understand the subtle meanings behind every step of a business process or behaviour encountered along the way. Ultimately, the owners are responsible for the outcome of the deal, therefore is it sensible that they take the lead and let the advisors assist them in this process.

- 'Lack of clarity in the execution of the integration process': The post-merger integration is known for being one of the major challenges for any M&A deal. Perhaps one of the most common yet predictable mistakes made is the absence of a clear implementation strategy that will ultimately lead to a successful execution of the deal. In pharmaceuticals, the task becomes particularly complex when also R&D programs do require integration. Often this process drags a lot of energy from the base business or, even worse, it goes on for too long thus causing frustration across the organisation. Uncoordinated actions, poorly managed systems migrations or contradictory communications to customers knock the business and undermine the core leaving the door open for competitors take advantage of. Nevertheless, a poor execution of an integration process can cause a steep increase in the actual costs of integration from which it may be difficult for the business to recover from in the next years. A careful preliminary assessment can help identify key employees, crucial products and projects, critical processes, bottlenecks, current capacity versus resources needed, etc. to design a realistic plan for implementation along with a efficient communication strategy.

- 'Cultural challenges': This is a factor that brings several risks to the integration and beyond. If leadership does not address cultural matters in a timely manner (that is how people feel about the new environment and how they will be cooperating in the future in key areas such as R&D, marketing and sales), this may cause little by little huge frustration across the entire organisation. Companies often take too much time to design and implement new organizational structures, whilst the most talented individuals and key personnel rather quickly leave. High-potential human resources, historical knowledge and competencies represent a loss from which the business will hardly recover. A proper strategy based on the new cultural values set for the newly formed organisation should be conceived sooner rather than later for deployment with the endorsement and support of senior leadership and buy-in from all key people within the business.

- 'Valuation and negotiation errors': This is a very common issue in those industries where high acquisition premia are paid, such as in Pharmaceuticals as we will discover in the following Chapter. The risk of a wrong evaluation may lead to financial losses which sometimes may be hard o recover

from for a newly formed venture. Sometimes it may be worth considering the assessment of alternative solutions such as being a sale target instead of a buyer, which may prove more profitable in the long run.

With such a large number of M&A deal failures, it is always a good idea to have a contingency plan in place to action when and if appropriate. Sometimes external factors may change the conditions of the business environment without the possibility to control or influence them. The best approach in these situations is to deploy a plan B to avoid any further losses. No businesses will ever have 100% guarantee their deal will be successful, however business owners, advisory firms and all relevant personnel involved in this type of activities should be at least aware of the most common pitfalls if they wish to increase their chances of success.

2. M&A in the Pharmaceutical Industry

As stated before, the pharmaceutical industry is one of the 'first industries' when it comes to mergers and acquisitions, both in the amount of money spent and the number of deals recorded. Whilst small, albeit significant acquisitions have now become an integral part of business operations in Pharma, the competitive landscape is continuously changed by large, industry-shaping deals that profoundly affect the market.

We now live in an era whereby the M&A activity can be considered as a standard component of the 'business model' in the strategy of a company, where it plays a fundamental role both in the short as well as the long run. In this industry, M&A's help ensure incumbents can leverage on the the R&D knowledge of the acquired targets and grow, by diversifying or revamping their product pipelines in order to become sustainable, remain competitive or enter new markets.

Over the recent years, a **growing trend** has been observed in this industry with an increasing number of mergers and acquisitions taking place across all geographies and therapeutic areas, thanks to a particularly favourable Regulatory environment, convenient interest rates and important tax reforms as explained before. The experts predicts that this trend is expected to keep growing over the years to come.

In particular, the segment of **Consumer Healthcare and Over the Counter (OTC)** medicines also recently experienced large, game-changing transactions between some of the key players in the market such as Merck & Bayer in 2014 for US$ 14.2 billion and Boehringer & Sanofi completed in 2017 for 21.8 billion asset swap and Novartis & GSK in 2018 for GBP 9.2 billion. As further indicated and analysed later on in this paper, a consolidation of the consumer health and OTC market is expected in the years to come with local brands being replaced by global brands benefitting from globalisation of consumer styles.

2.1 Pharmaceutical Industry overview

The contribution of pharmaceuticals to health and economic development globally is one of the reasons that make this industry one of the most valuable in the world. If we bring our attention to the biopharma and biotech sectors in particular, we notice that these two sectors have experience a constant growth over the past decade, primarily due to the increase in expenditures in healthcare globally (which on its own represents approximately '10.5% of the total gross domestic products, or GDP, of the world), the prevalence of chronic and transferable diseases and the increasingly ageing population worldwide.

An important factor which distinguishes the Pharmaceutical industry is the costly, risky and lengthy **research and development (R&D)** process performed by those operating in this sector with the aim to introduce new medicines into the market ("*The Pharmaceutical Industry in Figures*", EFPIA, 2018). On average, from the first synthesis of the new molecule to the moment a finished drug product is commercialized, 12 to 13 years will have elapsed. Perhaps not surprisingly, in 2016 the estimated costs of discovering and developing a new chemical entity (NCE) was around US$ 2.5 billion (*Di Masi et al., 2016*). Furthermore, it must also be taken into consideration that on average only 1 or 2 molecules will eventually complete successfully all the stages of the development process required in order to become a registered finished product out of approximately 10,000 substances synthesized in research centers and laboratories. In other words, this means that companies active in the field of research and development of new molecules do have only 0.01 or 0.02% chance of success in discovering a new drug.

The illustration below is a succinct representation of the several phases involved throughout the lifecycle of the research and development process in Pharma just to give the reader an indication of its length and complexity.

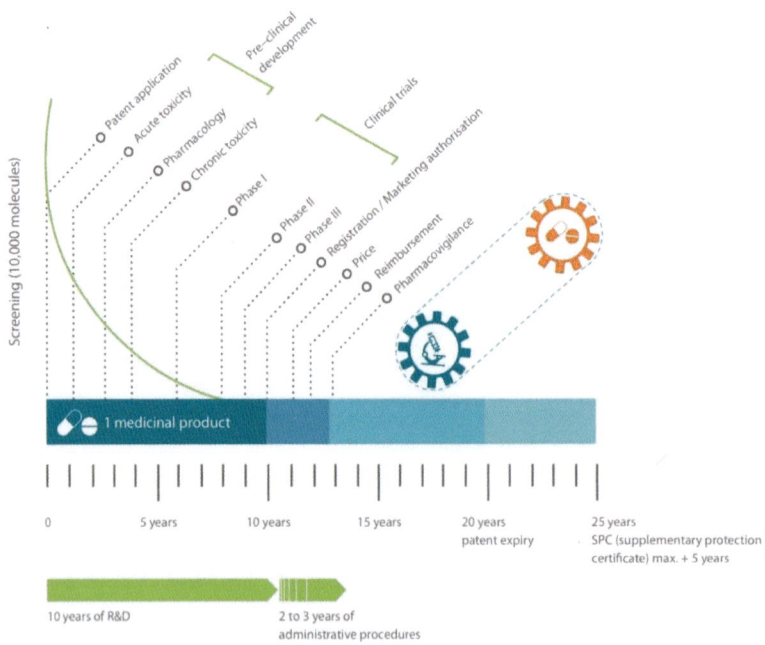

Source: The Pharmaceutical Industry in Figures, EFPIA, 2018

According to a recent research study conducted in 2018 by EFPIA (European Federation of Pharmaceutical Industries and Associations) from which this theory is mainly taken, the **value of global Pharma market** was estimated to be worth over US$ 850,000 million based on 2017 sales at the price at the factory (without including any other charges, such as delivery or subsequent taxes). According to the study, the largest markets in 2018 were the North America (including both United States & Canada) with a 48.1% share, followed by Europe (including Turkey and Russia) with 22%, Africa, Australia and Asia (excluding Japan) with 17%.

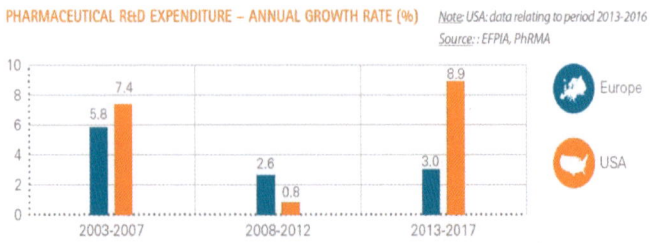

14

BREAKDOWN OF THE WORLD PHARMACEUTICAL MARKET – 2017 SALES

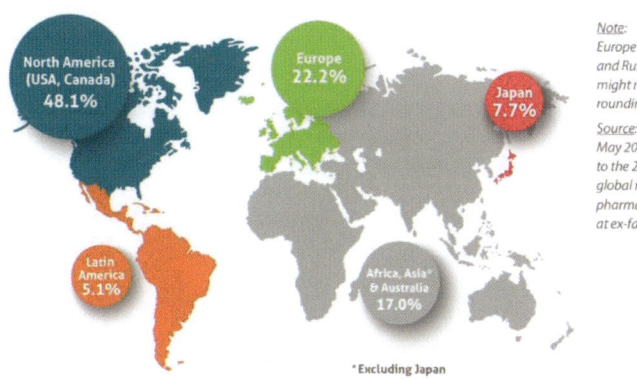

Note:
Europe includes Turkey and Russia; percentages might not add up due to rounding

Source: IQVIA (MIDAS), May 2018 (data relate to the 2017 audited global retail and hospital pharmaceutical market at ex-factory prices)

According to data provided via EUROSTAT, in comparison with other sectors such as high-tech or manufacturing, the pharmaceutical sector has the highest 'added-value per person employed' ratio on average. Furthermore, the pharmaceutical sector boasts also the topmost proportion of 'R&D investment compared to net sales' (15% in 2016 as shown in the graph below) respect to other high-tech industries, and over 19% of 'total business R&D expenditure' globally. Of note, the percentage of 'annual growth rate in R&D expenditure' reached

RANKING OF INDUSTRIAL SECTORS BY OVERALL SECTOR R&D INTENSITY
(R&D AS PERCENTAGE OF NET SALES – 2016)

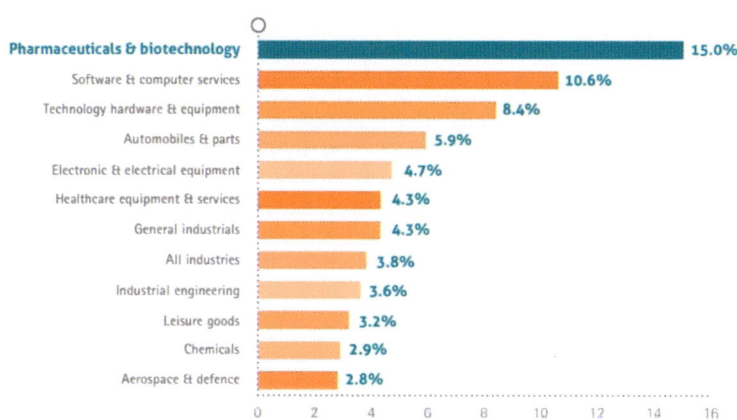

Note:
Data relate to the top 2,500 companies with registered offices in the EU (590), Japan (356), the US (837), China (327) and the Rest of the World (390), ranked by total worldwide R&D investment (with investment in R&D above € 21 million).

Source: The 2016 EU Industrial R&D Investment Scoreboard, European Commission, JRC/DG RTD

nearly 9% in the US over the period 2013-2016, showing once again the positive trend towards investments in R&D that business do make in this industry ("*The Pharmaceutical Industry in Figures*", EFPIA, 2018).

Indeed there is **rapid growth** in the market. According to the IQVIA Institute, a growth of 11.5% was recorded in the Brazilian market over the period from 2013 to 2017, followed by 11.0% growth in the India market and 9.4% growth by the Chinese market, compared to a market growth of 4.4% on average in EU (considering the top 5 markets only, i.e. United Kingdom, Germany, Italy, France and Spain) and 7.3% in US (*IQVIA Institute, March 2018*). The latter remain the markets with the highest 'annual growth rate percentage in Pharmaceutical R&D expenditure' (8.9% in the United States followed by 3.0% in Europe during the period from 2013 to 2017).

With particular regard to the **Consumer Healthcare** segment, the positive industry figures have been recorded over the recent years create a positive outlook for the companies who play in this arena. According to the IPSOS Survey conducted in 2017, an increasing healthcare awareness and self-care is characterising the consumers of this sector. The vast majority of them (about 77%) seems to be willing to take more control over decisions about their health, which means that the size of the market of over-the-counter (OTC) products and other non-prescription medicines may increase in its size in future. This may also be favoured by almost 2.4 billion more emerging middle-class consumers and 0.5 billion more 60+ aged people estimated by 2030 compared to 2015. On top of this, it has also to be noted that medicinal products whose patent is due to expire may become eligible for the so called 'Rx to OTC' switch (that is to move from being 'prescription only' to 'non-prescription'). This means these products will become available for self-medication as well as being marketable through more channels in future.

With all of the above taken into consideration, the forecasts for the Consumer Healthcare segment of the industry indeed look very bright. A consolidation of this market is expected in the upcoming years and acquirers in the industry are already keeping a close look at opportunities which may arise in this area in the near future.

2.2   The Drivers behind the Moves

Looking back and analysing the patters that have led to the raise in number of deals in the Pharmaceutical industry over the recent years is important to understand the drivers behind this growing trend.

In 2017, the M&A transactions were characterised by more conventional aspects such as the need for additional revenues to overcome the issue with mature assets, the pursuit of 'scale economies' to reduce cost of goods and be competitive in the market, the mitigation against the risk of disruption from new high-tech competitors, the ability to access additional product lines or geographies to mention a few. However, if we look at the deals announced in 2018 they seemed to be driven by rather different reasons. The trend seems now to have shifted towards **small and high-growth competitors** willing to sell their R&D discoveries to large Pharma players in order to leverage their sales and distribution capabilities (which they would not be able to build on their own due to high costs of infrastructures) and commercialise their products.

Generally speaking, one if not the most important factor to be considered as a driver for change is without doubts the 'significant costs' that incur in the drug development process as explained in the previous section: as mentioned, on average the estimated costs of discovering and developing a new chemical entity (NCE) is around US$ 2.5 billion and it takes 12 to 13 years from the first synthesis of the NCE to the moment a finished drug product is commercialized (*Di Masi et al., 2016*). Additionally, new products either must solve a problem for which a solution has not yet been found or else be better than what is already available in the market in order to become a marketable medicine and create value. Both **advancement of medicine**, along with the ever-

16

increasing **regulatory requirements** that pose greater challenges to Pharmaceutical companies, are the key drivers for the high costs of the development of a new drug product.

Another important aspect to consider is the advent of **generic medicinal products**. Due to lower reimbursement prices of generics, a major consolidation of leading generic drug providers has been seen over the past few decades. M&A activity largely affects also this segment with a number of industry-shaping transactions recorded in recent years, such as Teva's acquisition of Allergan's generic portfolio or End's purchase of US generic provider Par Pharma to mention a few.

The primary reasons why Pharma enterprises consider M&A can therefore be summarised as follows:

- Firstly, the market '**size requirements**' increased much faster than what a company could normally grow, therefore it has become difficult for any of the players in the market to succeed on their own without looking at economy of scale to reduce costs and increase the reach of their Supply Chain network.

- Secondly, M&A's allow companies to leverage on '**open innovation**' and build new platforms, aspects necessary to consider especially in the event of a patent cliff.

- Lastly, it is the '**nature of the industry**' which is known for being risk adverse and slow in responding to changes. Through M&A companies have the possibility to change the company's culture and better respond to major variation in regulatory requirements, critical in order to implement strategic changes within the organisation.

Efficient capital allocation is another important driver for M&A across the industry of principal applicability to the areas of R&D and manufacturing. Due to the size and complexity of organizational structures, large enterprises often do suffer lack of innovation when it comes to discovery of new molecules, technologies or processes. Having access to an ecosystem of entrepreneurs and venture capitals through **open innovation** strategies is an effective practice most companies follow in order to ensure a continuous flux of new ideas is coming in.

A recent research study conducted by McKinsey showed that the revenues' share obtained from innovations coming from outside of the Big Pharma companies has grown to 50% in 2016 ("*What's behind the pharmaceutical sector's M&A push*", *2018*).

In this article, the authors Bansal, De Backer and Ranade argument that in 2018 the enthusiasm of the pharmaceutical industry towards several emerging categories of drugs motivated pharmaceutical companies to look for suitable acquisition targets. The average premium paid for the pharmaceutical companies acquired in the first half of 2018 was approximately 60%, with around 90% taking place in the first quarter only. Interestingly enough, these deals primarily involved companies active in the area of immuno-oncology and rare diseases.

Furthermore, the same study has performed a research over the top 25 pharmaceutical companies under risk of patent expiries and estimated that the total value of income at risk over the next 3 years is approximately US$ 85 billion. This indicates a clear need from large companies to continually refresh their portfolios and pipelines in order to mitigate the risk of revenue decrease when patents expire and marketing authorisation holders lose their **exclusivity** right. This may sound a large sum, in reality however it still represents less than the turnover lost by companies because of expiration of patents in average the study says.

The American company Pfizer is one of the best examples to describe uncertainties and risks that **patent deadlines** bring to Big Pharma: their cardiovascular drug, Lipitor, whose revenues reached US$ 13 billion in 2007, today it has fallen to US$ 1.4 billion; again, their blockbuster Viagra, which was invoicing around US$ 7 billion in 2014, today it sits around at US$ 1 billion.

Another key motivator pushing companies towards the pursuit of a M&A deal is the need to capture synergies. This was the driver behind the acquisition of Takeda in May 2018 by the Irish Pharmaceutical company, Shire. The deal was undertaken with the expectation to generate, after only 3 years from completion, **annual cost synergies** of US$ 1.4 billion thanks to the complementary product pipelines of the two companies and their specular organisational structures.

In the study performed by McKensey in October 2018, midsize and large pharmaceutical companies were classified by margins and analyzed to evaluate the potential future opportunities. The spread obtained for companies with annual turnover exceeding US$ 1 billion spanned from EBITDA margins under 20% to more than 50%. The conclusions of the study suggested that pharmaceutical companies with 'high margins' have terrific opportunities to capture synergies through M&A activity ("*What's behind the pharmaceutical sector's M&A push*", *2018*).

2.3   Acquisition Premia in Pharma

Another very common aspect of the Pharmaceuticals which may be worth noticing is regarding the acquisition premia that has characterised majority of the transactions over recent years, and particularly in 2018 as briefly anticipated in the previous section.

According to a study conducted by the Bocconi Students Investment Club (BSIC) based on data sourced from Dealogic, acquirers in the Pharmaceutical industry were willing to pay on average in 2018 a premium of 81%. This value is more than double the premium paid on average in 2017, which instead was below 40%. Some of these 2018 transactions include the premium paid by Sanofi SA on Bioverativ Inc. equivalent to 63.78% and that paid by Celgene Corporation to acquire Juno Therapeutics, of 78.46% ("*2017 M&A Review and 2018 Breakthrough: the cases on the Pharma and TMT sectors*", *2018*).

As suggested by the study, these high levels of acquisition premium seem to be justified by a number of reasons:

- The **lack of highly profitable targets** causing strong pricing competition among the interested parties;
- The need to **grow inorganically** due to patent protection expiry of blockbuster products from big pharma players, as explained before;
- More generally speaking, the tendency that some distressed buyers may have to **overpay** when they are in need to revamp their product portfolios in order to remain competitive.

The above examples are better understood when looking at the context in which the involved parties operate: Sanofi's insulin-based blockbuster, Lantus, experienced a steep decrease in market share as the result of the introduction of other less expensive biosimilar versions in the market, creating a need for the French company to widen its product portfolio thus to mitigate the loss in sales; the decision of Celgene Corporation to purchase Juno Therapeutics, leader in the oncology area, was primarily driven by the patent expiry of its blockbuster, Revlimid, for patients with multiple myeloma.

The pattern has slightly changed over the years, according to the before mentioned McKinsey research by Bansal, De Baker and Ranade. When overcapacity was highly diffused across the sector in the early 2000s,

companies that created the most value were those who made the biggest deals. Nowadays however, pharmaceuticals have been more selective and those who have pursued small but cautious deals are the ones who have created the most value ("*What's behind the Pharmaceutical Sector's M&A push*", 2018).

2.4 Six Factors that contribute to Success in Pharma

Due to some of the aspects which characterise the Pharmaceutical industry such as the size of 'technical, regulatory and commercial' risks that companies in this sector face doing business, it is hard to guarantee success when it comes to mergers and acquisitions. In principle, if organisations followed a structured approach to managing deals, the chances of success could definitely improve in their favor. According to information sourced from the "Bain & Company Healthcare Manufacturer Merger and Acquisition Database", which records transactions occurring between pharmaceutical, medical device, biotech and diagnostic companies taking place over the period 1995-2008, nearly 60% of those generated greater returns in comparison to their peers from other industries.

According to the an article from Bain & Company from which the theory presented in this section is mainly taken, there are some patterns observed that contribute to success, as summarised below ("*Six ways to make healthcare deals work*", 2010):

- 'Frequent involvement in M&A activity'. The research performed by Bain & co. on what they name 'frequent acquirers' shows that over time organisations do have the ability to improve their skills in M&A integration activities based on previous, acquired experience thus extracting 'more value' and achieving bigger revenues than the market average. It seems also that organisations that execute 'more than 1 deal every 2 years' have built peculiar competencies they may be able to re-use to increase the chances of success in future transactions. 'Frequent acquirers' outperform the market. For example, in the past 20 years organisations such as Roche and Pfizer got successfully involved in more than twenty M&A transactions each. The process these companies have followed in most of their deals include an adequate initial investment in 'due diligence' activities along with the identification of areas of potential 'value creation'. After the deal, they have managed to combine assets and implement synergies effectively and as quickly as possible. Most importantly, they have ensured that the integration process have not distracted them from the business activities in their core.

- 'Focus on smaller acquisitions'. As indicated in some of the studies previously discussed in this paper, large deals do have less chances of success if compared to small, frequent acquisitions. In fact, companies that frequently acquire smaller assets seem to be able to deliver 'sustainable and higher' return as it was, for instance, for the Johnson & Johnson's business division 'Ethicon' which over a two-month period only (from December 2008 to January 2009) managed to acquire successfully 3 companies (Omrix, Mentor and Acclarent) in order to expand its portfolio. In general, these type of deals record returns over 3.5% compared with < 1% for larger deals.

- 'Valuing internal as well as external sources of innovation'. Particularly in the pharmaceutical sector where market leaders rarely control the majority of market share, industry leaders tend to follow a very methodical discipline in their programs regardless of whether they come from internal sources or external, such as when an 'open innovation' strategy applies. For example, following the acquisition of Wyeth, the market share of Pfizer grew in 2009 only to 11% with respect to the total market. This is because the merged business can produce only part of all the

innovation needed in order to drive growth in a sustainable manner, particularly for Pharmaceuticals. In order to ensure continuous growth, it is of essence that a company remains 'open to innovation' beyond its boundaries at all times.

- 'Investing when others do not'. It has been observed that during times of economic recession, the number of deals has substantially reduced with fewer players in the market taking the risk to bet on M&A activity. However, what has also been noticed for example after the economic downturn of 2001, that acquirers in the pharmaceutical sector who engaged in M&A during this period generated 'higher shareholder returns' compared with other industries. The reasons behind this result is attributable to the fact that these down cycles can help acquirers better mitigate the risks. As a matter of facts, whilst nearly half of the deals in the end fail to create value, this rate reduces to 30% during time of economic slowdown. And this is when Pharma businesses with high liquidity available can speed up their M&A strategy.

- 'Investing close to the core business'. Calling on the example discussed before, Johnson & Johnson's acquisitions added value because each of the purchased businesses fit complimentary with the existing company product portfolio. Recently leading pharmaceutical organisations have looked at M&A as a strategy to flower growth. Deal success seems to be correlated to how much the acquired asset is linked to the core business, since the ones with the highest rate of success seem to be those that invest in companies with assets and competences that strengthen their core.

- 'Approaching large deals selectively'. Lastly, in the pharmaceutical industry there seems to be a positive correlation between the size of the acquisitions and the returns obtained. In other words, the larger the deal, the higher the returns. Often, buyers save costs through consolidation of the supporting functions across the two organisations, such as commercial or other administrative departments, but most importantly it is by leveraging the strengths of the two businesses and building synergies where most of the value is created.

Albeit representing a useful guidance, by no means the above observations will give any guarantee of success in a M&A deal to acquires if followed. Each individual case presents its own complexity and therefore will have to be considered as stand-alone, as we will do with the case analysed in the next chapter.

2.5 Key Trends and Challenges ahead

Before moving on to the case study, it is important to spend a few words around key trends and challenges in the horizon. In addition to the patterns already highlighted, some trends soon become visible when we start paying greater attention to what the industry has been experiencing in recent years.

Whilst there is indeed a continue rise of M&A activity with regard to technology in healthcare, particularly around the need of automation and compliance in this ever-changing, highly demanding regulatory environment, combined with an increasing need to reduce costs and switch towards more value-based business models, interested buyers are also looking at companies that are flexible and able to adjust to new ways of working.

Thanks to populations with relatively disposable incomes, a lot of M&A activity is expected to take place in the US and Asia in future, according to the experts ("*Mergers and Acquisitions*", bakermckensie.com).

Differently to what we have seen thus far, vertical integration is expected to become a more common type of M&A in future, in order to help companies find opportunities for efficiencies areas such as logistics, manufacturing, etc. where growth as intended in the traditional way may become constrained.

The experts predict that due to growing **polical uncertainty** and **regulation complexity**, M&A activity in the healthcare sector is to reach its peak in 2020. New and cross-border investments will be affected in the future as pressure over trade continue, in particular between US and China. Brexit will also leave companies uncertain on possible deal activity between Europe and the UK, as the experts from Baker McKinzie firm explain.

Beside the political challenges, a lot of healthcare players will be facing the hurdles that the new General Data Protection Regulation (GDPR) measures brought in terms of **data protection**. This as well as similar regulations will force Pharma companies (who must collect data as part of the development process for new medicinal products) to protect data from their patients. Therefore the activities involved in the data collection process, particularly for clinical and safety purposes, will be hugely impacted by these new requirements, and so will be the upcoming M&A activities around this area moving forward.

The overall landscape for the years ahead gives a very complex picture to interpret, however only those who will have the ability to read through this complexity and decompose it into simpler items, will be able to affirm their leadership over competition tomorrow.

3. Case Analysis: GSK Consumer Healthcare

Only a month ago, two giants of the Pharmaceutical industry, the British GlaxoSmithKline plc and the American Pfizer Inc., announced the birth of a new, world-leading organisation by reaching a mutual agreement to merge their respective Consumer Healthcare businesses in to a brand new enterprise.

The newly merged entity will function under the name "**GSK Consumer Healthcare**" in all the geographies in which the two parent companies have a presence today, exception made for GSK's listed subsidiary in Nigeria.

According to the experts the new enterprise is already well-positioned to deliver an average annual **sales growth** of approximately 4%, improved cashflows and revenue growth thanks to leading 'Power Brands' in their combined portfolio, technology-based **innovation** and significant **cost synergies**. At the beginning of its journey, the company's combined sales is estimated to be approximately £9.8 billion and the transaction is predicted to generate by 2022 'total annual cost savings' of approximately £500 million. The newly formed company is intending to reinvest up to 25% of the cost savings into the corporation in order to bolster innovation as well as other growth opportunities ("*GSK and Pfizer to create a new Consumer Healthcare JV*", 2018).

Thanks to two highly complementary portfolios of well-known, highly profitable consumer health brands they bring together, such as Pfizer's Advil, Caltrate and Centrum and GSK's Voltaren, Sensodyne and Panadol, the newly formed enterprise is already a category leader in the areas of Respiratory, Pain Relief, Digestive Health, Therapeutic Oral Health, Skin Health, Vitamin and Mineral Supplements. The new corporation is expected to become the global leader in the market segment of Consumer Healthcare and OTC products with a 'market share' of 7.3% and have #1 or #2 positions in critical territories, such as US and China ("*GlaxoSmithKline plc and Pfizer Inc to form new world-leading Consumer Healthcare Joint Venture*", 2018).

Within 3 years from transaction closure, the intend is to split the corporation via a demerger of its equity interest from the parent companies and list "**GSK Consumer Healthcare**" in the UK equity market. The parent companies do expect to complete the majority of the integration over this period, thus to strengthen the business and its R&D portfolio. The strategic separation will permit the resulting enterprise to have adequate capital structures necessary in order to enable suitable capital allocation priorities and future investments. Thanks to its more durable cash flows, the new company resulting from this operation is expected to uphold 'higher leverage levels' than it could today.

On the board of the newly formed company, there will be 6 GSK directors, while Pfizer will have 3. **Emma Walmsley, current Chief Executive Officer in GSK,** will chair the business until separation.

Following the announcement, Emma Walmsley said to the press that the transaction with Pfizer represents a 'unique opportunity' to accelerate the work commenced eighteen months ago to improve GSK's long-term competitive performance and bring new discoveries and better healthcare products to people. She stated: "Through the combination of GSK and Pfizer's consumer healthcare businesses we will create substantial further value for shareholders. At the same time, incremental cashflows and visibility of the intended separation will help support GSK's future capital planning and further investment in our pharmaceuticals pipeline".

3.1 History of the Alliance

On 18th December 2018, the British GlaxoSmithKline plc and the American Pfizer Inc. officially announced for the first time their agreement to consolidate their respective Consumer Healthcare businesses into a new 'single entity'. The deal built on an earlier transaction in 2018 where GSK purchased Novartis' shares in the GSK-Novartis Consumer Healthcare business, thus acquiring full control of the venture.

Failed attempts to buy out the Pfizer Consumer Healthcare business had taken place throughout the year from several interested parties, including GSK withdrawing from an earlier auction process. In the end, the opportunity to sign an 'all-equity' deal opened the way to a new agreement, as Emma Walmsley said to the press. Following the announcement, GSK shares jumped 7% with Shareholders's enjoyment and continued to rise as much as 8.3% on the LSE whilst Pfizer shares rose about 1.2% in pre-market US trading as the result of this deal activity.

On 8th May 2019, GlaxoSmithKline plc announced that the **shareholder resolution** relating to the transaction was approved at the General Meeting held by GSK, with 99.85% of shareholders voting positively.

Prior to proceeding towards deal closure, the two parent companies had to request **approval from the European Commission (EC)** who initiated a market risk analysis to examin the effects that such an operation could have had on the markets in which they operate. Since both companies actively operate in the European Economic Area (EEA) in a number of over the counter (OTC) product categories (e.g. topical pain management, systemic pain management, cold and flu treatments, gastrointestinal treatments, nutrition and digestive health as well as sedatives and sleeping aids), the areas of concerns were many.

It was feared, in fact, that the combined business could reduce competition, for instance, in the sector of products for the control of topical pain, ending up with increasing the price in several European countries such as Italy and the Netherlands among others. To dispel the concerns of the European Commission on the creation of dominant positions, the companies proposed to abandon the ThermaCare business, a 'package' that will have to be sold to a buyer who will have to be approved by the Commission. The commitments that GSK and Pfizer have taken on include also the sale of a production plant located in the United States.

On 10th July 2019, the European Commission (EC) had given the green light to the formation of the venture **under the EU Merger Regulation**, conditioning it to full compliance with the commitments made by the two pharmaceutical companies.

Finally, on 1st August 2019 the two giants of the Pharmaceutical industry announced the birth of a new, world-leading organisation by reaching a mutual agreement to combine their respective consumer healthcare divisions into a new merged enterprise, with GSK controlling 68% of equity interest and Pfizer having the remaining 32%.

Brian McNamara, Chief Executive Officer (CEO) of GSK Consumer Healthcare, said: "Now that the deal has closed, our focus will be on completing the integration of these two businesses and leveraging their combined strength. With our portfolio of brilliant, science-based brands and strong talent and capabilities, we are well-positioned to create a world-leading consumer healthcare business with stronger sales, cash flow and contribution to earnings."

3.2 The Partner Companies

When analyzing a M&A deal, it is of outmost importance to consider also the potential areas of similarity and differences between the two merging companies in the attempt to understand whether they are an appropriate fit or not.

GSK and Pfizer are both large Anglosaxon multinational companies with global sites and operations spread all around the world. In their history, they showcase numerous successful mergers, acquisitions and other strategic alliances with international partners. The high level of in-house technical expertise, the continuous pursuit of innovation and the robust leadership and talent pool they can source from are certainly aspects critical to success that them both have in common. Furthermore, the comparable operating efficiency that the two companies present is also a reassuring measure of the similarity in their ability to deliver value to their shareholders.

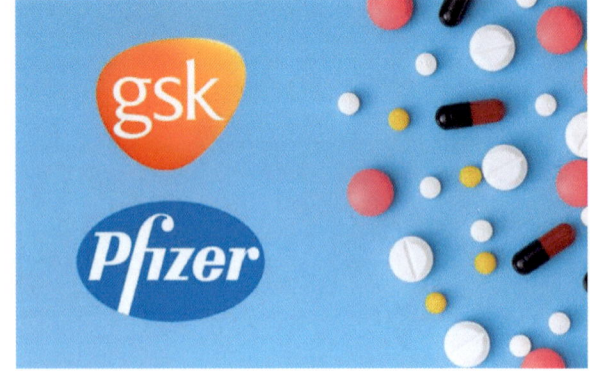

Now, even if from a preliminary analysis of the two partner companies there are positive feelings about this merger, whether the deal is eventually successful or not will depend on a more in-depth analysis of the case and, most importantly, on how well owners, managers and all of those involved in the execution of the deal, will be able to deliver a comprehensive integration plan that addresses the several aspects we discussed in this paper.

3.2.1 Glaxosmithkline Plc

GlaxoSmithKline plc (or GSK) is a British multi-national pharmaceutical company with headquarters in Brentford, London[4].

The history of this British Pharmaceutical giant is deeply linked with the topic of Mergers and Acquisitions. Its establishment in 2000 is the result of the merger between Glaxo Wellcome and SmithKline Beecham, with the newly formed company pursuing an intense M&A activity with other partnering companies following this major takeover, as shown in the Appendix.

Emma Walmsley, who is the very first female Chief Executive Officer in the history of GSK, became CEO on 31st March 2017. Since she took the leadership of the company, M&A activity has become a hot topic on the agenda of the group. A number of acquisitions have taken place during her mandate: from that with TESARO, an oncology biopharmaceutical company for US$ 5.1 billion, to the purchase of Novartis' share in the GSK-Novartis Consumer Healthcare venture for £9.2 billion, to a number of other non-core product divestments prior to entering into negotiations with Pfizer.

Some of GSK's top-selling products are Advair, Avodart, **Augmentin**, Flovent, the toothpaste **Sensodyne** and **Aquafresh**, the nicotine replacements Nicoderm and **Nicorette**, and the cold remedy Night Nurse. Of note, some of the legacy GSK products (such as amoxicillin and zidovudine to mention a few) are listed in the "World Health Organization Model List of Essential Medicines".

Today GSK offices are spread over 115 countries and the company employs nearly 100 thousand people of which approximately 12,500 are allocated to R&D. The company is listed on the London Stock Exchange (LSE) and is a component of the Financial Times Stock Exchange (FTSE) 100 Index. As of September 2019, the company has a market capitalisation of £87 billion which makes it one of the largest on the LSE today.

In 2018, the GSK group recorded over £30 billion in **turnover** with 2% **growth** over the previous year and an **operating profit** of over £5 billion. As of end of 2018, the GSK's earnings per share were 73.7 pence of a pound ("*2018 GSK Plc Annual Report*", *gsk.com*). The **stock price** of GSK is £17.06 as of 4th September 2019.

The GSK Consumer Healthcare division, which holds #1 positions in wellness across 36 markets with their comprehensive portfolio of trusted brands, including Sensodyne, Parodontax, Voltaren and Theraflu, generated sales of £7.7 billion in 2018.

In March 2018, GSK announced to have agreed with Novartis to buy out for £9.2 billion their 36.5% stake in their Consumer Healthcare business, in line with GSK's strategy that suggested the intention of the company to spin-off of its Consumer Healthcare division. Not long after, in December 2018 GSK again announced to have agreed with Pfizer to merge their Consumer Healthcare divisions in to a single entity, as discussed in this Chapter.

---

[4] The information and images captured in this paragraph is mainly sourced from the company's website, gsk.com, and wikipedia.org

3.2.2 Pfizer Inc.

Pfizer Inc. is an American pharmaceutical company with headquarters in Manhattan, New York City, and R&D headquarters in Groton, Connecticut (U.S.)[5].

The company is one of the largest pharmaceutical companies worldwide to be listed on the New York Stock Exchange (NYSE). In 2018, Pfizer ranked #57 on "the Fortune 500 list of the largest United States corporations by total revenue" (Fortune.com).

Like its partner GSK, also Pfizer has a long history of Mergers and Acquisitions recorded since its establishment in 1849, as shown in the Appendix A. Among these, the successful acquisition of Wyeth in 2009, King Pharmaceuticals in 2010 and the Small Molecule Antibiotic Division of AstraZeneca in 2016.

The company develops and manufactures pharmaceutical drugs and vaccines for a large span of therapeutical areas, such as neurology, immunology, cardiology, oncology and endocrinology. Their products pipeline comprehend well-known brands such as **Lipitor** (atorvastatin) for lowering LDL blood cholesterol, **Celebrex**, an anti-inflammatory drug, and the renowned **Viagra** (sildenafil) for erectile dysfunction.

In 2018 Pfizer reorganised its business into three separate units: Innovative medicines, Generic established medicines and off-patent drugs and Consumer healthcare.

As indicated in the Annual Report of the company, in 2018 Pfizer recorded over US$ 53,647 billion in revenues with 2% growth over the previous year and over US$ 11,153 billion in Net Income. The company's earnings per share (EPS) was US$ 1.87 at the end of 2018 ("*2018 Pfizer Inc. Annual Report*", August 2019). The stock price of Pfizer as of 4th September 2019 is $35.83.

Most of Pfizer's revenues come from its core prescription drugs, particularly through the sell of its blockbusters Lipitor (a **cardiovascular drug**), Viagra (for erectile dysfunction) and Lyrica (for cholesterol medication). The first two have experienced a huge fall in their revenues in recent years following the expiry of their patents (Lipitor went from US$ 13 billion in 2007 to US$ 1.4 billion today and Viagra from US$ 7 billion in 2014 to US$ 1 billion) and the latter is in line to face a similar decrease in sales over the next years due to its recent patent expiry on 30th June 2019.

As the result of this, in order to mitigate the issues of patent deadlines and revenues loss, in October 2017 Pfizer began a strategic review of their Consumer Healthcare business with the expectation to raise capital in the order of magnitude of US$ 15 billion. Several possible options were considered as part of this exercise, spanning from the spin-off of the division to a divestment though direct sale. In October 2018, Reckitt Benkiser expressed interest in bidding for the division with Johnson & Johnson (J&J), Sanofi, Procter & Gamble (P&G) and GlaxoSmithKline also being interested. Finally, in December 2018, Pfizer and GlaxoSmithKline announced to have agreed on the merger of their Consumer Healthcare businesses in to a single, combined entity as discussed in this Chapter.

---

[5] The information and images captured in this paragraph is mainly sourced from the company's website, pfizer.com, and wikipedia.org

3.3 The Basis of the Strategic Alliance

On 1st August 2019 GSK and Pfizer have finalised the agreement to create a new combined entity under the name of "**GSK Consumer Healthcare**" where GSK will control 68% of equity interest and Pfizer the remaining 32%, with the latter contributing through its consumer healthcare division's resources to the GSK consumer healthcare business in exchange of equity shares.

Whilst completion of the transaction has taken place on this day, the transfer of relevant assets will only occur when receipt of appropriate market-specific approvals will be received, as per the local requirements applicable in each of those jurisdictions in which the company will do business.

The newly formed corporation will operate in all territories where either or both parent companies do business today (exception is made for GSK's subsidiary in Nigeria only). Out of the scope of the venture are some of the GSK's Consumer Healthcare products proposed for divestment, such as Horlicks (a sweet, malted, milk hot drink) as well as other products from its Consumer Healthcare nutrition pipeline.

As mentioned before, the transaction was subject to GSK's shareholders agreement (which took place on 8th May 2019 during a GSK General Meeting with 99.85% of shareholders voting in favour to the company formation) as well as certain anti-trust authority prior approvals such as that from the European Commission (obtained on 10th July 2019 under certain conditions as agreed with the interested parties) prior to being finalised.

In the new business, GSK will have a major stake in the control of the combined enterprise company through the board of the newly combined business (formed by 6 GSK directors and 3 Pfizer directors), whilst Pfizer will enjoy customary minority shareholder protections. Within 3 years from transaction closure, the parent companies intend to split the corporation via a demerger of its equity interest from the parent companies and list GSK Consumer Healthcare on the UK equity market. Until separation, **Emma Walmsley** is the Chair whilst **Brian McNamara** is appointed as designate Chief Executive Officer and **Tobias Hestler** as a designate Chief Finance Officer.

The following conditions were agreed by both parties under the expert advice from their respective legal representatives and advisory firms involved in the negotiations, such as J. P. Morgan Cazenove and Citi, as reported to the press ("*GlaxoSmithKline plc and Pfizer Inc to form new world-leading Consumer Healthcare Joint Venture*", 2019):

- For the 'first five years from transaction closure', GSK will be the only party to have decisional power to determine whether and when the demerger can be indicated. Additionally, GSK will also have the right to sell its shares (all or in part) in a 'contemporaneous IPO' (Initial Public Offering) during this time. If a separation takes place over this period, Pfizer will also be allowed to take part either through the divestment of its equity interest (32%) or its sale in an IPO.

- Once the 5-year period elapsed, both parent companies will have the same power to decide if and when to initiate the demerger of the company. From this point onwards, if Pfizer initiates the demerger, GSK will have the option to buy out all of equity interest from Pfizer in the business (that is the remaining 32%) at fair market value. Of note, GSK will solely be able to purchase the totality of the remaining share, but not only part of it.

- Furthermore, from the 15th year of transaction closing, GSK will be allowed to purchase the remaining equity interest from Pfizer (i.e. 32%) at fair market value. Again, this condition applies to the purchase the totality of the remaining share only.

Regardless of terms and circumstances, in the event of separation the company will incur borrowings as to result in 3.5x-4.0x of net debt to the aggregate of their last 4Q's Adjusted EBITDA. The profit of this recapitalisation will be divided by the two parent companies proportionally to their respective equity interests prior to the separation. In any case, GSK will preserve the privilege to decide the proposed 'dividend policy' of

the new enterprise if the Adjusted profit 'pay-out' ratio of the new company in the last 4 quarters is between 30% and 50%.

Certain precautions were also put in place during the negotiations to protect Pfizer's rights from a potential withdrawal or delay of the deal (e.g. a 'break fee' payment of US$ 900 million by GSK). Until separation, the new merged enterprise does not forecast to carry any 'external debt' and its financial statements will be consolidated in GSK group's ones.

3.4 Financial Considerations

A brief analysis of some financial aspects of the GSK Consumer Healthcare deal has been performed as part of this study to support the evaluation of the transaction also from a monetary point of view and to provide a more comprehensive and broader picture.

The following valuation is based on information retrieved from "Circular to Shareholders and Notice of General Meeting" issued by GSK on 2nd April 2019 regarding the proposed Consumer Healthcare M&A with Pfizer Inc. The table shows a breakdown of the revenue and adjusted operating profit of the two companies for the year 2017 and 2018. For comparison purposes, it has been taken the average 2017 exchange rate GBP to USD of 1.30 proposed by GSK during the announcement in December 2018.

Tab. 1 Financial Figures[6]

	2018	2017
GSK Consumer Healthcare		
Revenue	7,055	7,110
EBIT	1,238	1,254
Pfizer Consumer Healthcare		
Revenue	2,758	2,668
EBIT	553	462

If we want to assess the enterprise value of the two companies, we can use the *method of comparables* referencing for instance to the valuation multiples **EV/Revenue** and **EV/EBIT** (*"Corporate Finance"*, J. Berk & P. DeMarzo, 2017).

Since the two companies operate in the same business, we can use the same sector ratios as shown below:

$$\text{Multiples 1:} \frac{EV}{Revenue} = Average\ in\ the\ sector = \left(\frac{EV}{Revenue}\right)_{AVG}$$

---

[6] Figures are rounded up and adjusted at best to include items in scope of the merged entity only. For the purposes of the evaluation, British Pound Sterling (GBP) is the preferred currency used in this financial analysis. Therefore all US$ figures have ben converted into GBP using an exchange rate of 1 GBP = 1.30 US$ as the average conversion rate in 2017 used in the "GSK Circular to Shareholders and Notice of General Meeting" from where this data is sourced.

28

$$\text{Multiples 2:} \frac{EV}{EBIT} = \text{Average in the sector} = \left(\frac{EV}{EBIT}\right)_{AVG}$$

Therefore, the 'Enterprise Value' of the firm will be the sum of the stand-alone value of the two companies plus any synergy which can be expected:

$$EV = EV_{GSK} + EV_{Pfizer} + Synergy$$

Hence we obtain a value which is between EV_1 and EV_2 as calculated below:

$$EV_1 = \left[\left(\frac{EV}{Revenue}\right)_{AVG} x \left(Revenue_{GSK} + Revenue_{Pfizer}\right)\right]$$

Since synergy estimated by the parent companies in their announcement thanks to cost savings gravitates around £500 million, this value can be added to the EBIT sum of the two companies also:

$$EV_2 = \left[\left(\frac{EV}{EBIT}\right)_{AVG} x \left(EBIT_{GSK} + EBIT_{Pfizer} + Synergy\right)\right]$$

For the solely purpose of this exercise, the relevant multiples for 19 of the main competitors across the industry have been calculated in the table that follows, giving a resulting average industry value of 4.17 for EV/Revenue and 20.33 for EV/EBIT.

As a result of this, the Enterprise Value of the new entity, based on the average of the industry, is estimated to be between:

EV_1 = £ 41 billion (considering EV/Revenue multiples)

EV_2 = £ 47 billion (considering EV/EBIT multiples)

Tab. 2 Industry Multiples[7]

2018		
Company	EV/Revenue	EV/EBIT
Johnson & Johnson	4.38	18.79
Novartis	3.62	12.96
Novo Nordisk	6.31	14.29
Sanofi	3.14	23.14
Bayer	2.36	23.81
Merck	5.19	23.19
AstraZeneca	5.16	41.13
Eli Lilly	5.64	32.27
AbbVie	5.25	26.26
Bristol-Myers Squibb	3.70	13.56
Lundbeck	2.77	9.57
Herbalife Nutrition	2.03	15.50
Reckitt Benkiser Group	4.20	17.21
Procter & Gamble	4.36	44.91
Gilead Sciences	3.54	8.82
Amgen	5.50	11.94
Celgene	3.88	10.64
GlaxoSmithKline	3.09	17.17
Pfizer	5.20	21.15
Average	4.17	20.33

---

[7] Data sourced from macrotrends.com

Of note, the ratios obtained for both companies in the two years considered are similar. This shows a comparable operating efficiency between the two firms involved in the deal.

If we now attempt to valuate the percentage of contribution of each parent company to the combined business based on the financial information disclosed by the companies to shareholders ("*GSK Circular to Shareholders and Notice of General Meeting*", 2017), the weight of each company in the new entity can be calculated as follows:

- Method 1:

$$GSK = \frac{Revenue_{GSK}}{Revenue_{GSK} + Revenue_{Pfizer}}$$

$$Pfizer = \frac{Revenue_{Pfizer}}{Revenue_{GSK} + Revenue_{Pfizer}}$$

- Method 2:

$$GSK = \frac{EBIT_{GSK}}{EBIT_{GSK} + EBIT_{Pfizer}}$$

$$Pfizer = \frac{EBIT_{Pfizer}}{EBIT_{GSK} + EBIT_{Pfizer}}$$

Therefore, the rations above provide the weight of GSK and Pfizer in the new created company by using both revenue and the EBIT:

Tab. 3 Equity Interest Valuation

	2018	2017
GSK Consumer Healthcare		
Revenue	72%	73%
EBIT	69%	73%
Pfizer Consumer Healthcare		
Revenue	28%	27%
EBIT	31%	27%

Based on these calculations from the past two years, GSK was contributing with a weight between 69% and 73% in the new created business, while Pfizer was accounting with a value between 27% and 31%, values which are close enough to the equity interests agreed by both parties as part of the deal (that is 68% for GSK and 32% for Pfizer).

With all relevant conversion rate fluctuations being considered, along with any additional specific information which might have been excluded from this brief evaluation, overall we can assume that from a financial point of view, a fair percentage of equity interest was attributed to each parent company when signing off the deal.

3.5 Main Benefits and Synergies

In theoretical terms, GSK Consumer Healthcare as a single entity blends together both core strengths and capabilities of its parent companies. A number of mutually beneficial advantages have the potential of being achieved through this company formation, spanning from the merger of two already existing portfolio's of well-known products and trusted brands globally that the newly formed business is inheriting from each parent company, to entering one of the largest, fastest-growing industries with a considerable market share, to the possibility to expand into whitespaces thanks to their large R&D capability.

Some among the most important synergies each parent company can achieve through the strategic alliance and the benefits they bring, have been assessed in more detail and summarised in this section in no particular order.

- **Key core capabilities**: The new company can benefit from its parent companies' respective Power Branding, consumer understanding and technical expertise. Additionally, the combined business will inherit from each parent company best-in-class R&D capabilities, including worldwide R&D sites such as Warren (US), Weybridge (UK), Nyon (Switzerland), Hyderabad (India) and Shanghai (China), as well as large, highly efficient manufacturing facilities, as in Pittsburg (US), Durgavan (Ireland), Guayama (Puerto Rico), Montreal (Canada) and Aprilia (Italy).
- **Expansion into new categories**: Following on the above, through exploitation of its R&D capabilities, the newly formed entity has the potential to develop innovative products and enter new product categories across a variety of therapeutic areas of Consumer Healthcare and OTC sector. The newly formed company is intending to reinvest up to 25% of the cost savings into the corporation in order to bolster innovation as well as other growth opportunities which probably moving forward will bring the business on the frontline of research and development in a sector where low-prices often prevail over high-technological innovation.
- **Cost synergies and operational efficiencies**: In the new enterprise, each partner acquires the possibility to leverage on a dense supply chain network with high bargaining power to realise more value. As announced by the companies, GSK Consumer Healthcare is predicted to generate about £500 million of total annual cost savings by 2022. Considering the large scale of the business on a global level, there is a positive outlook on the cost synergies which are likely to be achieved either through an increased level of production (i.e. economy of scale) or the production of complementary services (i.e. economy of scope) as well as through consolidation of the supporting functions across the two existing organisations, such as commercial or other administrative departments.
- **A broad geographical presence**: Through the venture, each partner can leverage strong presence into some of the largest, fastest-growing and most promising Consumer Healthcare and OTC (Over-The-Counter) markets internationally such as the UK, US, Canada, Australia, Italy, France, India, Brazil, Mexico and Indonesia just to mention a few. A world map of has been created to illustrate the existing global coverage of Pfizer Inc., GSK plc or both, thus to give an idea of the global footprint which the newly formed business can leverage today. As mentioned

32

before, through the combined business the parent companies have increased their market share to 7.3% over competition and have already reached #1 or #2 market share positions in critical territories such as US and China. Of note, based on 2017 results, 29% of their combined sales come from the Emerging Markets.

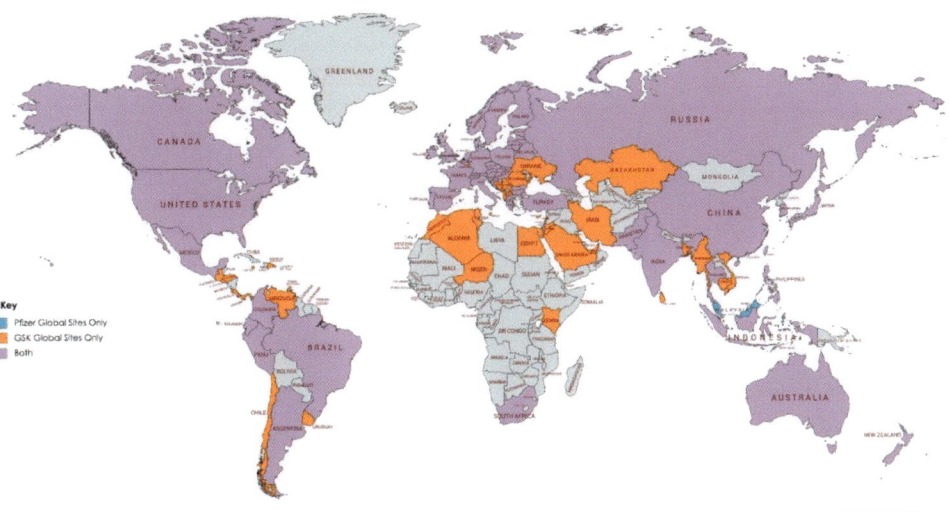

- **A strong Product portfolio**: Thanks to the a wide range of well-known products and highly trusted brands globally inherited from each parent company, the newly formed business is well suited to become soon the leader in the Consumer Healthcare and OTC market. They commercialise products across several therapeutic areas including Pain Management, Digestive Health, Dietary Supplements, Respiratory, Personal Care and more. As shown in the table below, the combined portfolio is already #1 in several product categories such as Pain Relief, Multivitamins (VMS), Respiratory and Skin Health with brands such as **Voltaren**, **Panadol**, **Sensodyne** and **Chapstick**. Two products, **Advil** for pain management and Centrum, a multivitamin product, are among the top 10 OTC brands in the world today.

Based on the observations above, the combined business appears to have all it is required to become a world-leading enterprise in the Consumer Healthcare sector and to deliver considerable value to their shareholders. However, further considerations for instance on the value of performance improvements which may be required to upgrade those capabilities as well as the challenges that all other post-merger integration activities bring, must also be taken into account prior to draw some final conclusions.

1. Nicholas Hall's DB6 Global OTC Database, 2017. For Skin Health, share and ranking based on OTC derms category. 2. GSK analysis is based on Nielsen, IRI and Euromonitor data

3.6 Principal Risks and Uncertainties

The value that mergers and acquisitions bring to partner companies is often counterweighted with threats which may emerge for each partner. Some of the most common pitfalls which may lead to failure in M&A deals were discussed in greater detail in section 1.4. Failure to produce and execute a comprehensive integration plan, lack of establishing appropriate level of controls, losing focus are all applicable to this case and therefore will require close attention by the relevant parties.

In addition to these, the principal risks and uncertainties relevant to the newly formed entity and its parent companies in the context where they operate and their impact over their ability to achieve both strategic and financial objectives, are further analysed and summarised in this section in no particular order.

- **Compliance with laws and regulations:** This applies throughout the several functions that constitute the business, from R&D, manufacturing, quality, safety, supply chain and distribution, to marketing and sales. An intense regulatory activity is expected over the following months for the relevant departments involved with compliance matters in order to ensure that the legal transfers of responsibility as applicable are notified and, where necessary approved, in all territories where the products are marketed. The risk of non-compliances may affect any existing products in the market as well as new products in development phase where additional costs and time required prior to launching may be required. Considering the size of potential impact of this threat, a separate mention must be made to the risk of failing to comply with tax laws as per applicable legislation in the jurisdictions where the company operates (including for example Anti-bribery & corruption, ABAC) principles and standards. Besides the tangible costs which could negatively affect financial results, this may also impose serious damage to the reputation of the parent companies and their relationships with customers and regulatory bodies worldwide.

- **Product Quality, Crisis Management and Supply Continuity**: Another major threat particularly common during the delicate integration process and knowledge transfer between the

34

two merging companies worth noticing is presented by inadequate governance and quality controls for example in supply chain, manufacturing and distribution of products. The potential risk posed by failures to deliver continuous supplies of products or by the inability to react efficiently and timely to a crisis incident such as product recalls, which may occur particularly during the integration phase, is also a threat to be taken into consideration. In this category also falls the risk of failing to appropriately collect, review or report adverse events (AE's) from all potential sources and to act in a timely manner on any relevant findings, thus impacting patient safety and imposing serious risks to public health.

- **Information Protection**: The risk that both parent companies may incur if information is 'accidentally disclosed' to unauthorised parties, or if electronic information management systems fail or are corrupted during the integration process, represent a threat for both parent companies involved, for example for intellectual property (IP) reasons. Considering the size of the parent companies and the complex IT technological infrastructures they have in place today which will require transfer of information and integration, this is definitely a concern which should be carefully assessed. The risk of information protection can be also extended for example to failing to maintain adequate oversight over all third parties involved in the integration process, such as large consulting firms who may be tasked to facilitate this process.

The risks and uncertainties briefly touched in this section represent only some of the threats the company may encounter along the integration process which may obstruct their way towards the achievement of financial results and other strategic objectives. A thorough risk analysis and mitigation plan addressing each of the potential risks identified by the relevant functions within the company is expected to be performed by the management team. As the result of this, appropriate actions will have to be put in place in order to ensure appropriate **risk management** and protection of shareholders' interests.

Considering the extensive experience in M&A that both parent companies have developed over the years and the number of deals they have taken well to completion in their history to date, we have every confidence to believe they will be able to apply the same level of success in the management of this deal too.

Conclusions

We cannot conclude this paper without addressing again how much of a critical tool for strategy implementation M&A is across all industries, and particularly in Pharma. Today, M&A represent a common element in the 'business model' of any pharmaceutical company, necessary to get rapid access to innovation, expand business product pipelines or streamline manufacturing operations.

The pursuit of the right deal is fundamental in order to bring 'game-changing' moves in the strategic plan of a business and prepare organisations to face new challenges. But how do we determine what is the **right deal**?

The empirical evidence discussed in this paper is important because it helps the reader understand that there is no mathematical formula that can help answer this question. Like any other strategy, acquisitions cannot be considered just 'good or bad'. Each M&A opportunity must have its own **strategic rational** and the organisations involved in the process must ensure they have the necessary skills to execute its implementation, if we want it to be successful.

As we have discovered in this paper, acquisitions do create more value for the selling company's shareholders than for the acquirers'. It is only when the performance of the acquired company increases by more than the value of the premium paid that we see value creation in a deal. The best acquirers build systematic institutional skills in defining their M&A strategy, managing their reputation as an acquirer and consistently looking for performance improvement opportunities beyond those estimated before the deal was complete.

And **managers** play a fundamental role in this process since they can help ensure value is created through a strategic rational that falls into one of the six archetypes as described in this paper. The measure of success of a M&A also critically depends on their ability to make accurate estimates of the revenue and cost improvements that the acquired company can realise under their leadership, taking also into consideration costs and challenges that an integration process brings. Managers should also be reminded that what interests the stock markets is only the actual impact of acquisitions on the 'intrinsic value' of the combined entity.

Furthermore, **post-merger integration** activities do also play a critical part in the success story of a deal. It is by avoiding the most common pitfalls that companies encounter during an integration process and appropriately mitigating the risks that the management team can have better chances to realise the 'full value' of a deal for their shareholders.

Despite the challenges that come with this activity, companies in the pharmaceutical segment in particular cannot ignore M&A strategies as a mean to growth. The 'right deal' can offset the challenges companies face as the result of the increase in regulatory complexity, the rise of competition, price pressures or lack of innovation. If the acquisition is aligned with the broader strategy of the business and appropriate measures are taken before and after the transaction, a pharmaceutical company can go hunting for targets with confidence. Deals hit the mark when they enable value creation not only for the shareholders but also for all stakeholders of the process, including investors, employees, physicians, distributors as well as patients.

As we learnt from this paper, the best approach towards creation of value in mergers and acquisitions sits around 3 main pillars: a true 'strategic rational', a comprehensive 'integration plan' and the 'organisational culture' kept at the heart of the deal. These concepts can be applied to the GSK Consumer Healthcare case, the example of horizontal merger we studied.

Based on the observations made in the relevant sections, the combined business appears to have all it is required to become a world-leading enterprise in the Consumer Healthcare and OTC sector and to deliver significant value to the shareholders. However, in order to ensure value creation in the years to come, both GSK and Pfizer will need to contribute in equal part to this process by providing their own capabilities and resources for the benefit of the respective partner as well as leveraging the other's strengths and long experience they have gained to date with regard to M&A's. Moreover, by remaining faithful to their strategy and culture as well as by following a structured and pragmatical approach in their integration process, we can have confidence to believe that the 'right deal' has been signed and the road to success for this newly formed business is straight ahead.

Bibliography

Aamir M., Ahmad S.T., Mehmood Q.S., Ali U., Jamil R. A., Zaman K. (2014). The Challenge of Patent Expiry: A Case Study of Pharmaceutical Industry. Mediterranean Journal of Social Sciences.

Amihud Y., Lev B. (1981). Risk Reduction as a Managerial Motive for Conglomerate Mergers. The Bell Journal of Economics, 12(2): 605-617.

Anderson H., Havila V., Nilsson F. (2013). Mergers and Acquisitions: The Critical Role of Stakeholders. New York: Routledge.

Bansal R., De Backer R., Ranade V. (2018). What's behind the Pharmaceutical Sector. McKinsey

Bain.com

Bakermckenzie.com

BBC.com

Bloomberg.com

Bsic.it

Bowman C.H. (2013). The role of corporate culture in mergers and acquisitions. Mergers and acquisitions: Practices, Performance and Perspectives. NOVA Science Publishers.

Burger L., Revill J., Miller J. (2018). GSK buys out Novartis in $13 billion consumer healthcare shake-up. Reuters.

Chesbrough H.W., Appleyard M.M., (2007). Open Innovation and Strategy. University of California – Berkeley

Chesbrough H.W. (2003). The Era of Open Innovation. MIT Sloan Management Review

Çilhoroz Y., Songur C., Gozlu M., Konca M. (2016). Mergers and acquisitions in pharmaceutical industry as a growth strategy: an investigation upon practice. International Journal of Business and Management. Vol. IV(3), pp. 1-12.

Church J. (2008) Conglomerate Mergers, Issues in Competition Law and Policy. ABA Section of Antitrust Law, 2: 1503-1552.

Clougherty J.A.. Duso T. (2009). The Impact of Horizontal Mergers on Rivals: Gains to Being Left Outside a Merger. Journal of Management Studies, 46(8):1365-1395.

Cnn.com

Damodaran A. (2005). The Value of Synergy. Stern School of Business.

Danzon P., Epstein A., Nicholson S. (2007). Mergers and Acquisitions in the Pharmaceutical and Biotech Industries. Managerial and Decision Economics, 28(4-5):307-328.

Demirbag M., Chang-Keong NG., Tatoglu E. (2007). Performance of Mergers and Acquisitions in the Pharmaceutical Industry: A Comparative Perspective. Multinational Business Review, 15(2):41-61.

Depamphilis D.M. (2012). Mergers, Acquisitions and Other Restructuring Activities, Sixth Edition, UK: Academic Press.

Di Masi J., Grabowski H.G., Hansen R.W. (2016). Innovation in the pharmaceutical industry: New estimates of R&D costs. Journal of Health Economics 47(2016):20-33.

Di Minin A., De Marco C.E., Marullo C., Piccaluga A., Casprini E., Mah dad M., Paraboschi A. (2016). Case Studies on Open Innovation in ICT. JRC Science for Policy Report

Ehm W., Uhlaner R., West A. (2012). Taking a Longer-Term look at M&A Value Creation. McKinsey Quarterly

Ec.europa.eu

EFPIA.eu

Federfarma.it

FT.com

FTPress.com

Fortune.com

Globallegalchronicle.com

Gsk.com

Haberberg A., Rieple A. (2008). Strategic Management: Theory and Application, Oxford: Oxford University Press.

Harding D., Rovit S. (2004). Mastering the merger: Four critical decisions that make or break the deal. Harvard Business Press.

Harrigan KR. (2003). Vertical Integration, Outsourcing, and Corporate Strategy. Washington: Beard Books.

Herper M. (2012). Three Lessons From GlaxoSmithKline's Purchase Of Human Genome Sciences. Forbes.

Herper M. (2017). GlaxoSmithKline Appoints Big Pharma's First Woman Chief Executive. *Forbes.*

Investopedia.com

Jung J. (2002). Creating Breakthrough Innovation During a Pharmaceutical Merger or Acquisition. IBM Institute for Business Value Manuscript.

Karanpuria R. (2014). Mergers and Acquisition. Project on Mergers and acquisitions in Pharmaceutical Sector, National Law School of India University.

Katsanis L.P. (2015) Global Issues in Pharmaceutical Marketing, UK: Routledge Publishing.

Koller T., Goedhart M., Wessels D. (2015). Valuation - Measuring and Managing the Value of Companies. McKinsey and Company.

Kollewe J. (2014). GlaxoSmithKline faces criminal investigation by Serious Fraud Office. *The Guardian.*

Kumanpartners.com

Lodorfos G., Boateng A. (2006). The role of culture in the merger and acquisition process: Evidence from the European chemical industry. Management Decision 44(10):1405-1421

Marks M.L., Mirvis P.H., R. Ashkenas (2014). Making the most of Culture Clash in M&A. Leader to Leader.

Macrotrends.net

Mitchell M.L., Stafford E. (2000). Managerial Decisions and Long-Term Stock Price Performance. Journal of Business 73

Mittra J., (2007). Life Science Innovation and the Restructuring of the Pharmaceutical Industry: Merger, Acquisition and Strategic Alliance Behaviour of Large Firms. Technology Analysis and Strategic Management, 19(3):279-301.

Moeller S.B., Schlingemann R.M., Stultz. Do shareholders of acquiring firms gain from acquisitions?. Working Paper 9523, National Bureau of Economic Research, 2003

Morresi O., Pezzi A. (2014). Cross-Border Mergers and Acquisitions: Theory and Empirical Evidence. Palgrave New York: Macmillan.

Murphy A., Ponciano J., Hansen S. (2015). The World's Biggest Public Companies. Forbes.

Neville S. (2012). GlaxoSmithKline fined $3bn after bribing doctors to increase drugs sales. The Guardian.

Nytimes.com

Pharma.elsevier.com

Pilsbury S., Meaney A. (2009). Are Horizontal Mergers and Vertical Integration a Problem?. Joint Transport Research Centre, Discussion Paper No. 2009-4.

Pfizer.com

Pharmaceutical-technology.com

Pharmastar.it

Pg.com

Pwc.com

Ravenscraft D., Long W.F. (2000). Paths to Creating Value in Pharmaceutical Mergers. University of Chicago Press.

Rehm W., Siversten C. (2010). A Strong Fundation for M&A in 2010. McKinsey on Finance.

Rehm W., Uhlaner R., West A. (2012). Taking a long-term look at M&A value creation. McKinsey Quarterly.

Ridley K. (2014). UK fraud office liaising with China on GSK bribery case. Reuters.

Sirower M., Sahna S. (2006). Avoiding the Synergy Trap: Practical guidance on M&A decisions for CEO's and Boards. Journal of Applied Corporate Finance 18, no. 3

Seth S. (2019). Top reasons why M&A deals fail. Investopedia.

Statista.com

Thedrum.com

Theguardian.com

Thepharmaletter.com

Thomas K., Schmidt M.S. (2012). Glaxo Agrees to Pay $3 Billion in Fraud Settlement. The New York Times.

Wang JX., Chiu YS. (2013). Conglomerate Merger Control: From the Continents to a Small Economy. Frontiers of Law in China , 8(2):305-334.

Wikipedia.org

Zook C., Allen J. (2010). Profit from the core: A return to growth in turbulent times. Harvard Business Press.

Zhu P.C., Hilsenrath P.E. (2015). Mergers and Acquisitions in U.S. Retail Pharmacy. Journal of Health Care Finance, 41(3):1-20.

Appendices

A. Acquisition History Diagrams[8]

<u>GlazoSkithKline</u>
- SmithKline Beecham Plc (Renamed 1989)
  - *SmithKline Beckman (Renamed 1982)*
    - SmithKline-RIT (Renamed 1968)
      - *Smith, Kline & French (Reorganized 1929 into Smith Kline and French Laboratories)*
        - French, Richards and Company (Acquired 1981)
        - Smith, Kline and Company
      - *Recherche et Industrie Thérapeutiques (Acquired 1968)*
    - Beckman Instruments, Inc. (Merged 1982, Sold 1989)
      - Specialized Instruments Corp. (Acquired 1954)
      - Offner Electronics (Acquired 1961)
    - *International Clinical Laboratories (Acquired 1989)*
    - *Reckitt & Colman (Acquired 1999)*
- Beecham Group Plc (Merged 1989)
  - *Beecham Group Ltd*
    - S. E. Massengill Company (Acquired 1971)
    - C.L. Bencard (Acquired 1953)
    - County Chemicals
  - *Norcliff Thayer (Acquired 1986)*
- Glaxo Wellcome
  - *Glaxo (Merged 1995)*
    - Joseph Nathan & Co
    - Allen & Hanburys (Founded 1715, acquired 1958)
    - Meyer Laboratories (Merged 1978)
    - Affymax (Acquired 1995)
  - *Wellcome Foundation (Renamed 1924, merged 1995)*
    - Burroughs Wellcome & Company (Founded 1880)
    - McDougall & Robertson Inc (Acquired 1959)
- Block Drug (Acquired 2001)
- CNS Inc. (Acquired 2006)
- Stiefel Laboratories (Acquired 2009)
- Laboratorios Phoenix (Acquired 2010)
- Maxinutrition (Acquired 2010)
- CellZome (Acquired 2011)
- Human Genome Sciences (Acquired 2013)
- GlycoVaxyn (Acquired 2015)
- Tesaro (Acquired 2018)

---

[8] Sourced from Wikipedia.org

Pfizer (Founded 1849 as Charles Pfizer & Company)
- Warner-Lambert
    - *William R. Warner (Founded 1856, merged 1955)*
    - *Lambert Pharmacal Company (Merged 1955)*
    - *Parke-Davis (Founded 1860, Acq 1976)*
    - *Wilkinson Sword (Acq 1993, divested 2003)*
    - *Agouron (Acq 1999)*
- Pharmacia (Acq 2002)
    - *Pharmacia & Upjohn (Merged 2000)*
    - *Pharmacia (Merged 1995)*
    - *Farmitalia Carlo Erba*
    - *Kabi Pharmacia*
    - *Pharmacia Aktiebolaget*
    - *The Upjohn Company (Merged 1995)*
    - *Monsanto (Merged 2000, divested 2002)*
    - *Searle (Merged 2000)*
- Esperion Therapeutics (Acq 2003, divested 2008)
- Meridica (Acq 2004)
- Vicuron Pharmaceuticals (Acq 2005)
- Idun (Acq 2005)
- Angiosyn (Acq 2005)
- Powermed (Acq 2006)
- Rinat (Acq 2006)
- Coley Pharmaceutical Group (Acq 2007)
- CovX (Acq 2007)
- Encysive Pharmaceuticals Inc (Acq 2008)
- Wyeth (Acq 2009)
    - *Chef Boyardeed*
    - *S.M.A. Corporation*
    - *Ayerst Laboratories (Acq 1943)*
    - *Fort Dodge Serum Company (Acq 1945)*
    - *Bristol-Myers (Animal Health div)*
    - *Parke-Davis (Animal Health div)*
    - *A.H. Robins*
    - *Sherwood Medical (Acq 1982)*
    - *Genetics Institute Inc. (Acq 1992)*
    - *American Cyanamid (Acq 1994)*
    - *Lederle Laboratories*
    - *Solvay (Acq 1995, Animal Health div)*
- King Pharmaceutical (Acq 2010)
    - *Monarch Pharmaceuticals, Inc.*
    - *King Pharmaceuticals Research and Development, Inc.*
    - *Meridian Medical Technologies, Inc.*
    - *Parkedale Pharmaceuticals, Inc.*
    - *King Pharmaceuticals Canada Inc.*
    - *Monarch Pharmaceuticals Ireland Limited*
- Synbiotics Corporation (Acq 2011)
- Icagen (Acq 2011)

- NextWave Pharmaceuticals, Inc (Acq 2012)
- Innopharma (Acq 2014)
- Redvax GmbH (Acq 2014)
- Hospira (Spun off from Abbott Laboratories 2004, Acq 2015)
    - *Mayne Pharma Ltd (Acq 2007)*
    - *Pliva-Croatia*
    - *Orchid Chemicals & Pharmaceuticals Ltd. (Generics & Injectables div, Acq 2009)*
    - *Javelin Pharmaceuticals, Inc. (Acq 2010)*
    - *TheraDoc (Acq 2010)*
- Anacor Pharmaceuticals (Acq 2016)
- Bamboo Therapeutics (Acq 2016)
- Medivation (Acq 2016)
- AstraZeneca (Small molecule antibiotic div, Acq 2016)

We declare that this book is the result of our own work and all sources of reference are acknowledged in full.
The EUREKA! Consulting Solutions group.

Printed in Great Britain
by Amazon